My wife and I became Christia[ns?] were in our early twenties at th[e time? We had been] married for two years. In those [years we learned] some foundational things about walking with Jesus that have consistently produced good fruit in our lives. We have noted that the majority of Christians today do not seem to understand some of these foundational things. These things do not seem to be widely taught today.

One of these things was described to us as "Walking in the Spirit." There are probably other things that it could be called. What it meant to us was that we would be empowered by the Holy Spirit to live a powerful Christian life and do everything that Christ taught His disciples if we "plugged into" who and what Christ had accomplished by His death and resurrection. "Plugging into Christ" was accomplished by "keeping our eyes on Jesus." In other words, focusing on Christ allowed the Holy Spirit to minister the things that Christ had accomplished to us on an ongoing daily basis.

It wasn't enough to simply believe in Christ and His work for us on the cross and then not be mindful of it in daily living. Reception of grace through the power of the Spirit worked as we kept our focus on Christ and what He had done for us.

This worked well for us and we prospered in our faith in Christ and grew in our capacity to do the things that Christ taught His disciples. We grew as Christians in every way possible. We still had some doctrinal misunderstandings but we were plugged in to Christ and life was flowing to us. He was the vine and we were His branches in an experiential way.

"I am the vine, you are the branches; he who abides in

Keep Your Eyes Fixed on Jesus

Me, and I in him, he bears much fruit; for apart from Me you can do nothing. (John 15:5)

We were living, abiding in Him, by keeping our focus upon Him. As a result, we were bearing fruit. We were growing in every respect in relationship to Him. We were being set free from sinful tendencies, demonic activity, strengthened in our love for God and one another and being changed into His image. Unfortunately, we allowed ourselves to become *unplugged*.

In the late 1980s, we were exposed to a teaching that refocused us on ourselves rather than on Christ. This teaching has been called "Roots and Fruits." The "Roots and Fruits" teaching would be best described as trying to find the roots of our problems and that would enable us to deal with the fruit of our problems. We accepted it without questioning probably because the culture has similar ideas about finding the psychological reasons why you have problems. We were not equipped at that time to ask the important discernment questions about this teaching. We would ask these questions today:

Did Jesus Christ teach His disciples to pursue ministry in this fashion? Did He demonstrate this way of ministry Himself? Would any of the Apostles have known anything about this way of doing ministry? Are there any examples of doing ministry in this fashion revealed in the New Testament?

Because we didn't know to ask these questions, we bought into this way of doing ministry and begin to pursue "finding the roots of our problems." After a number of frustrating years in this unending negative pursuit, my

Keep Your Eyes Fixed on Jesus

insightful wife Ann said something that got my attention and made me rethink what we were doing. She said "We have become navel gazers." I didn't understand what she meant and made a joke of it. I replied something like…"Do you mean like watching ships go by?" I was thinking she had said "naval" rather than "navel." She didn't laugh and said with a serious tone... "No, I mean navel gazers" and pointed to her navel. She went on to say "We were taught to look to Jesus, to keep our eyes on Him and now we are looking inside ourselves to solve problems. I can't remember when I last felt happy but I am sure that it was before we started looking for roots."

She was right. We had unplugged from the power source and we were trying to fix the fallen old man. We were trying to get the fallen flesh to act as if it was the redeemed spiritual nature. We had not made application of Paul's warning about the flesh and spirit being contrary to each other. Paul writes:

But I say, walk by the Spirit, and you will not carry out the desire of the flesh. For the flesh sets its desire against the Spirit, and the Spirit against the flesh; for these are in opposition to one another, so that you may not do the things that you please. (Galatians 5:16-17)

Earlier in that same book, Paul had reproved the Christians in Galatia by writing:

Are you so foolish? Having begun by the Spirit, are you now being perfected by the flesh? (Galatians 3:3)

It is obvious that it is possible to return to the flesh. This is the Greek word "sarx." It is found 130 times in the New Testament. It often means "the fallen human nature" We

Keep Your Eyes Fixed on Jesus

had begun by the Spirit and He has focused us on what Christ had done for us. As a result, we had walked in the power of the Spirit and lived victoriously. We had lost that focus and now we were focusing upon ourselves and nothing worked. We were frustrated and discouraged.

Ann and I abandoned introspective pursuits that day and refocused ourselves on Christ. Our joy in being Christians returned and our fellowship with Christ was renewed. We have seen abundant fruitfulness in our service to Him and we have continued to grow in grace with Him at the center of our lives. Indeed a few years after this, the Lord placed me in a fruitful situation and I saw thousands of young people receive Christ as Savior and Lord.

A few years beyond that situation, the Lord validated this focus on Him and He showed me how to do healing ministry. Since that time, I have traveled to more than 300 churches worldwide and seen approximately 30,000 healings and miracles. I believe that this is largely because of receiving grace through a Christ centered focus.

Recently on Facebook, I responded to a question in a thread in which I broached the subject of focus. I had a great deal of positive response to two paragraphs that I wrote there. At the same time, my wife, Ann had been asking me to write on the subject for several months for use in her service to Christ. She presently is the head of an online organization of 300 Christians. She found herself teaching about this repeatedly. She said that she needed something to help people understand. This was not easy to write as there is much that can be said about this and much that can be misunderstood. So here is how it is written. In this document, there is first an explanation

Keep Your Eyes Fixed on Jesus

of what focus is and some passages from the New Testament to explain it. Following this, there is a section that includes more information about focus and its effect on us but is not elaborated upon. In order to keep this document short enough to be useful for my wife (and other people,) I had to settle on what to expand in explanation and what not to expand.

Focus, for the purposes of this discussion, is defined as:

Our focus is the ongoing object of our thoughts. It is not our thoughts themselves. It is subject and object of what we find ourselves studying, dwelling on, concentrating upon, and meditating on momentarily or habitually. Our focus is the core, the essence, the spirit and heart of our thoughts. It is the origination point, the undergirding, the framework, the foundation and controlling element behind our thoughts.

Some of the key phrases and words in the New Testament that describe focus are "fixing your eyes upon," "looking for," "beholding," "set your mind on," "keep seeking those things," "meditate upon," and "study." Additionally, the New Testament has 22 verses where both the word "flesh" and the word "spirit" are found and are set against each other as opposites and often are in contexts that are warnings to Christians.

The New Testament teaches that there are only two kinds of focus in a variety of places. It also shows that each of these foci has a predictable affect on the believer. Some of the comparisons of focus in the New Testament are "good" or "bad," "spirit" or "flesh," "heavenly" or "earthly," "light" or "darkness," "life" or "death," "conformity" or

Keep Your Eyes Fixed on Jesus

"transformation." For example, the apostle Paul makes these two foci clear in this statement. He writes:

For the mind set on the flesh is death, but the mind set on the Spirit is life and peace... Romans 8:6

Our inner nature will predictably reflect the focus on the mind. If the focus is fleshly, the inner nature will experience the spiritual condition of *"death"* meaning that we will be cut off from the life of God, even before bodily death happens. This is not God cutting us off from His presence and power but rather a failure to plug into His provision in Christ for us. The old man, the flesh, the "sarx," will be in control as if the new man in Christ was unplugged and turned off. What exists "in Christ" for us is not received automatically. It must be appropriated.

If the focus is on the Spirit, spiritual things and things above, then the inner nature will reflect life and peace. Our new nature will be plugged in, switched on and empowered by the life of God. The old man will reflect the truth of his death and burial with Christ in baptism. In the same way that a dead man does not experience temptation and does not sin, the fallen nature, the old man will be switched off. The new nature that is in the image of Christ will rule through Christ. Paul writes a similar truth in the book of Colossians. He writes:

If then, you have been raised with Christ, keep seeking the things above, where Christ is, seated at the right hand of God. Set your mind on the things above, not on the things that are on earth. Colossians 3:1-2

Our focus on *things above*, particularly Christ Himself, enables us to experience the power of our identification

Keep Your Eyes Fixed on Jesus

with Christ in death, resurrection and ascension. Paul describes that heavenly, spiritual focus in two phrases… "seeking the things above" and "setting your mind on the things above."

The context of these two verses goes back into the previous chapter. For instance, Paul reminds us in Colossians 2:20 that "you have died with Christ." As a result of this eternal truth of identification with Christ at the cross, we should not submit to earthly religious rules of behavior because they have no value against fleshly indulgence.

Focusing on religious rules of behavior simply does not work to change behavior because rules are imposed from the outside and do not change us inwardly. Rules and law are a focus on the flesh. Trying to keep rules actually insures that the new nature is turned off. This is because trying to keep rules is an earthly focus.

Either the old man or the new nature in Christ will reveal itself in attitudes and behavior. Focus determines which nature is in control. Paul tells us in the verses quoted above that our focus on "things above" does have power over the flesh. It does have power to change our inner condition. It switches on and empowers the new nature in Christ. We live as those who have been raised with Christ. In other words, we live in resurrection power while still on the earth. This is available only through maintaining a spiritual focus.

The Lord Jesus Christ powerfully reveals this truth in a context where He speaks over and over again about the two possible foci. This is found in Christ teaching to His

Keep Your Eyes Fixed on Jesus

disciples on the mount that has been called "the Sermon on the Mount." This passage begins with this verse. *And when He saw the multitudes, He went up on the mountain; and after He sat down, His disciples came to Him. And opening His mouth He began to teach them, saying, (Matthew 5:1-2)*

Christ taught His disciples. It is a teaching to His disciples intended for them to be able to nourish grace in their lives and to learn what pleases the Father. In this teaching, Christ warns His disciples by saying:

"Beware of practicing your righteousness before men to be noticed by them; otherwise you have no reward with your Father who is in heaven." (Matthew 6:1)

Christ then illustrates the desire to "be noticed of men" in three areas of Christian life; giving, prayer and fasting. Christ reveals that it is a temptation for a believer to focus on building a personal reputation for spirituality by giving, praying or fasting. It is quite easy to see this bad focus working in the Church at times in our day.

One focus is to be "seen of men." as you give, pray or fast. In other words, the desire to build a reputation for spirituality is an earthly focus of the flesh. Christ teaches His disciples that there will be no reward from the Father for doing these things if we have such a poor focus. On the other hand, Christ tells us (as His disciples) if we do these things to the Father "in secret," then we will have an "open reward" from the Father. In other words, those who have the right focus, the right motive, for doing these spiritual things, will receive a reward from God for doing them.

Keep Your Eyes Fixed on Jesus

Christ then shifts the emphasis slightly in this passage to the subject of finances. He tells us again there are only two possible foci that will determine our inner condition and our behavior. He tells us not to lay up treasures on earth but in heaven.

"But lay up for yourselves treasures in heaven, where neither moth nor rust destroys, and where thieves do not break in or steal; for where your treasure is, there will your heart be also." (Matthew 6:20-21)

What we find ourselves thinking about continually reveals the nature of our focus. Our focus will be on earthy treasure or heavenly treasure. Our focus reveals where our treasure is located and that reveals the condition of our heart. In the next verse, Christ says:

The lamp of the body is the eye; if therefore your eye is clear, your whole body will be full of light. But if your eye is bad, your whole body will be full of darkness. Matthew 6:22-23a

Christ uses "the eye" to represent focus. He tells us of the two possible foci and describes them as "clear" and "bad." A "clear" focus predictably results in our bodies being "full of light." A *bad* focus results in our bodies being "full of darkness." What we experience inwardly… "death" or "life and peace" are a result of and is controlled by what we focus upon.

In the next few verses, in this context about finances, Christ gives believers additional information about these foci. He describes two possible foci as "masters." They are "God" and "mammon." "Mammon" means "money." Christ states that we can have only one as a master. This

Keep Your Eyes Fixed on Jesus

is another way of saying that we can focus only on one thing at a time. Either God is your master or money rules you. You will serve and focus on one or the other.

Christ reveals that anxiety is the inner condition of a person that has a focus on money rather than God. Ongoing anxiety over finances (or anything else) is a reliable sign that we have a bad focus. A proper spiritual focus will bring life, peace and light. This is true no matter what we face. There is so much more here in this passage that could be written but this discussion must remain focused on the subject of focus.

Everyone at all times has a focus. This focus may change many times an hour or remain reasonably constant. Our focus may be weak or intense. What determines our feelings, our ongoing inner condition, is our focus. If our focus is good, then our feelings will also be good. If our focus is bad, then our feelings will also be bad. Therefore, if an otherwise healthy person, has anxiety, fear or other negative feelings happening, it is likely to be because they have a bad focus.

Changing their focus will change their inner condition. If there is need for deliverance from the power of the enemy, then a proper focus on Christ as Deliverer, will allow the Holy Spirit to bring freedom to someone experiencing more than natural anxiety and fear. Deliverance from the power of the enemy often occurs when a spiritual focus is obtained.

Creating a disciplined lifestyle that purposely nourishes the new nature by strengthening the spiritual focus is important. No perfection is necessary as we learn and grow in our focus upon spiritual things. In the same way a

Keep Your Eyes Fixed on Jesus

baby cannot focus his eyes properly at birth but does so as they mature, we need to learn to focus at first but a good focus on the right things should become a habit.

Focus is always a matter of choice. It is not dictated by outward circumstances no matter how bad the circumstances might be. While negative circumstances seem to demand our attention and focus, the reality is that we can still maintain a proper focus.

Two people with similar negative circumstances will interpret the same negative facts differently and have differing reactions inwardly if their focus is different. The negative facts do not determine their inner experience. How they see the negative facts will be the determining factor of their inner condition. That will be determined by their focus.

Likewise, two people with similar positive circumstances may interpret the same positive facts differently and have differing reactions inwardly if their focus is different. One may focus on a negative comparison with someone else. For instance, perhaps I have gotten a large raise in pay in my work situation but someone else in the same office got a much larger raise in pay. Despite the fact of my situation greatly improving, I become angry inwardly because of my focus on the other person. However, if I maintained my focus upon Christ, I could feel grateful both to Christ and to my employer. Instead of feeling angry because someone else got a bigger raise, instead I could be glad for them and grateful that they received a blessing from the Lord as well.

Negative focus with the corresponding negative feelings is often a habit pattern that can be changed. We need to

Keep Your Eyes Fixed on Jesus

remember that a negative focus, no matter what the circumstances, does nothing to change the circumstances and will create an inner condition that will make things worse. A spiritual focus, in bad circumstances, allows faith in Christ to receive a potential answer to a difficult situation. A spiritual focus in a good situation allows us to respond in the proper manner to the Lord and to other people.

We must seek to capture all things that seek to make our focus earthly and upon ourselves. A joyful and peaceful inner nature and fellowship with the risen Christ is the daily reward of keeping a spiritual focus. Transformation of the entire person, spirit and soul, into the image of Christ, is the reward of maintaining a spiritual focus over days, months, years and decades. Paul writes:

> *But we all, with unveiled face beholding as in a mirror the glory of the Lord, are being transformed into the same image... 2 Corinthians 3:18a*

As we focus our eyes upon Christ the Lord, we are transformed into the same image. The work of the Holy Spirit is released in us to make us like Christ in every way as we focus on Christ. We grow up into His image fully. In the same way that a baby boy is both like and unlike his grown father, we are born into the image of Christ inwardly but this image needs to grow up fully into the image of Christ in every way.

Keeping our Eyes Fixed on Jesus
There are many things that draw our attention away from the most important things in life. It is necessary to continue to remind ourselves of what the inspired New Testament writers teach us to do about these distractions

Keep Your Eyes Fixed on Jesus

and what the potential reward is in maintaining a proper focus. The writer of Hebrews offers us this encouragement:

> *Therefore, since we have so great a cloud of witnesses surrounding us, let us also lay aside every encumbrance, and the sin which so easily entangles us, and let us run with endurance the race that is set before us, fixing our eyes on Jesus, the author and perfecter of faith, who for the joy set before Him endured the cross, despising the shame, and has sat down at the right hand of the throne of God. Hebrews 12:1-2*

In order to understand these verses in context, the passage does reveal that the writer of Hebrews is referring to a metaphorical race that requires endurance, perhaps drawing this illustration from the Greek marathon. There is so much content in these two verses that it seems wise to consider them thought by thought. This is the first thought in the two verses:

Therefore, since we have so great a cloud of witnesses surrounding us…
By the use of the word *therefore*, the writer is revealing that he is making summation and conclusion from the statements that he has made previously in the previous chapter of Hebrews. (Readers should be aware that there were no chapter divisions or verse divisions in the original manuscripts. They were added later in the history of the Church for the purposes of making translation easier and more accurate.}

The writer of Hebrews then refers to "the cloud of witnesses surrounding us." These witnesses are now watching believers in their race. In Hebrews Chapter 11,

Keep Your Eyes Fixed on Jesus

the writer lists many heroes found in the Old Testament who lived by faith. These heroes are now watching those who believe in Christ run this metaphorical race. Among these heroes that lived by faith, he mentions in particular Abraham and Moses who are among the witnesses now watching us.

...let us also lay aside every encumbrance...

The writer of Hebrews, referring back to the Old Testament heroes, encourages believers to do what those heroes of faith have done and to lay aside anything that would be a hindrance in succeeding in this race. This statement does not seem to be addressing sin in a believer's life as the passage will say something specifically about sin in the next phrase. It seems to be addressing lifestyles that are overly complex, that are dealing with too many things to allow time and energy for focus on the most important things.

These kinds of overly busy lifestyles are apparent in any age. The picture that the writer is offering us is a marathoner who is trying to run the race with a heavy pack on his back and bulky things in his hands. If he finishes the race at all, it will be with great difficulty. Obviously the wise thing to do is to shed every encumbrance. Many times the really important eternal things are neglected in favor of what seems to be of passing importance. In the next phrase, the writer of Hebrews says:

...and the sin which so easily entangles us...

Here the writer addresses the subject of sin in a believer's life. He describes sin *as* "easily entangles us."

Keep Your Eyes Fixed on Jesus

In terms of a race, the picture would be like a vine tying up the feet and ankles of someone trying to run, tripping them and causing them to fall. The necessity of not letting sin tie us up seems clear as we would not finish the race.

There is encouragement here in that the writer says that we can potentially lay aside this sin. We will not succeed in laying aside this sin by simply denying that it is a problem. We lay aside entangling sin by repentance from it, confessing it, receiving forgiveness of it and focusing on the divine fact of our old man's crucifixion and burial in Christ). He continues by writing:

…and let us run with endurance the race that is set before us…

This race is metaphorical and does symbolically represent the entirety of a believer's life. The writer tells us that this race will require *endurance* which does remind of the Greek Marathon. It does appear also that all believers are in this race whether or not they recognize it. This race is *set before us* by God. Now we arrive at a key point in this passage. The writer states:

…fixing our eyes on Jesus…

This statement, like other places in the New Testament, tells us that the ultimate focus of a Christian is on Jesus Christ Himself. This focus is not momentary or occasional but is for the entire metaphorical race. This focus is for a lifetime. The Greek phrase that is translated as "fixing our eyes" in a very literal sense means:

…to look away from all else.

Keep Your Eyes Fixed on Jesus

The Louw-Nida Greek-English Lexicon of the New Testament says that it *means:*

...to keep thinking about (Jesus), without having one's attention distracted.

The Thayer Greek-English Greek-English Lexicon of the New Testament says that it means:

...to turn the eyes away from other things and fix them on (Jesus)...

The ultimate, ongoing and enduring focus of a believer's life should be Jesus Christ. Our thoughts and attention should be on Him. Nothing else will be adequate as a primary focus. No other focus will produce in the believer what God wishes. A runner can testify that it is impossible to run in a straight line and with balance if your focus is on your own feet. Neither can you breathe properly while looking down. You must look outward to Christ in order to run the race properly and the Breath of God will sustain you.

The passage adds this modifying phrase that describes Jesus Christ:

...the author and perfecter of faith...

The Greek word that *author* is translated from is *archegos.* It means literally

...one who has gone first on the path.

This Greek word is sometimes translated as "leader," "prince," "pioneer," "originator," "founder," "initiator" or

Keep Your Eyes Fixed on Jesus

"author." This word does remind us that Christ is worthy of our apt attention, our focus, for the reason that He has gone first on this path of walking in the New Covenant and sets a perfect example for us of a man doing the will of the Father and empowered by the Holy Spirit. Beyond that, faith in Christ was the saving expression of all believers in the very beginning of their walks with God. It should be obvious that our Christian faith begins with seeing Christ through the Gospel.

The writer then tells us that Christ is "the perfecter of faith." The Greek word translated as "perfecter" is "teleiotes." This word literally means:

...one who makes possible the successful completion of something.

It is translated today as "perfecter," "finisher" or "consummator" in much older translations. This Greek word is only used once in the New Testament. It is specifically a designation, title or ministry of Christ Himself. Christ is the One who brings faith to its highest attainment, either in Himself as an example or in others through His High Priestly ministry of intercession that continually presents believers to the Father.

Christ makes possible the successful completion of our lifelong race. Setting our gaze upon Him without distraction makes sense in light of His importance as the One who has gone before and the One who will enable us to compete the race successfully. We are empowered to walk in grace by keeping our focus on Him. This enables us to emulate Him and be empowered to do the things that He taught His disciples. The writer of Hebrews continues by telling us of Christ's focus:

Keep Your Eyes Fixed on Jesus

...who for the joy set before Him endured the cross...

Christ had "joy set before Him" by the Father that enabled Him to endure the cross. Perhaps the event that has been called the Transfiguration was a joyful revelation of what the cross would accomplish and what resurrection from the dead would be like. Perhaps that event allowed Christ to focus beyond the sufferings of the cross. In any event, joy was set before Christ and the focus that this joy created enabled Christ to endure the cross. The next phrase describes what the cross was like for Christ. Christ endured the cross...

...despising the shame...

Jesus focused on the *joy set before Him.* This focus enabled Him to endure the humiliation of the cross. Proper focus allows the Holy Spirit to empower us to endure difficult times victoriously and brings us safely to the end of the race.

Christ has once, for all and for all times has crossed the finish line...

...and has sat down at the right hand of the throne of God.

While Christ has finished His own race successfully. He now enables us as the Finisher of our faith to complete ours. We plug into His capacity by focusing on Him. We receive the grace that we need to do all that Christ teaches His disciples. Jesus Christ Himself is the ultimate object of a proper focus. The Holy Spirit's main activity in believer's lives is to reveal Christ and make known what Father has provided in Him. When a believer focuses

Keep Your Eyes Fixed on Jesus

upon Christ, he powerfully aligns himself with the work of the Holy Spirit in his life. When that disciple determines to make Christ Lord in everyway and do what Christ teaches His disciples in the Gospels and elsewhere, the Holy Spirit greatly empowers that believer to succeed.

More Thoughts on Focus
No one thinks about God every moment. This is not what proper focus is about. When someone has developed and practiced a proper focus on Christ, even when their thoughts in dealing with the practical daily issues of life are not essentially about Christ, these thoughts will be filtered through and controlled by this undergirding knowledge of Christ. All the practical issues of life become spiritual when the focus remains spiritual.

This is not like secular positive thinking because that philosophy is simply encouraging concentrating on the best that human wisdom, religious flesh and the world has to offer. While this may help create a more positive inner nature, it does not activate and empower the new nature nor does it create faith in Christ and reception of His help.

It is not like New Age thinking or popular but cultic grace teachings. This approach does not deny the reality of sin, the fallen nature, sickness, bondage or death. It does not deny the reality. It simply denies the finality of these negative things because of what Christ has done.

Because we can only focus on one thing at time, proper focus is always outward to Christ and is not an appraising, introspective gaze into ourselves. Trying to analyze and appraise ourselves, find and fix problems in ourselves (including curses) is a powerless pursuit as it

Keep Your Eyes Fixed on Jesus

requires us to make ourselves the object of our focus. This self-focus effectively unplugs our new nature from the Spirit of Christ and allows the old man to surface and to reassert himself.

Introspection is a carnal, fleshly focus on the old man, the flesh, which will not lead to freedom but to more bondage. It is possible to take spiritual truths such as "our authority in Christ" and place such a strong emphasis on "our authority" and such a weak emphasis on "in Christ" to turn this truth into a powerless focus upon ourselves.

By keeping Christ as our focus, at the center of our thoughts, faith in Him is produced and we have an ongoing reception of what Christ has accomplished by His cross and resurrection. We abide in Christ. This activates and strengthens the new nature that is in the image of Christ and puts to death the old nature that was crucified with Christ. Sin loses its hold on us by abiding in Christ. Demonic activity against us is thrown into disarray and bondage is dispelled as we stay *plugged into* Him through focus.

The ability to focus continually on the right things, such as Christ, is strengthened by practicing meditation on and study of the New Testament. We don't study it just to obtain information. We study it to know Jesus Christ better. As we fill our mind continually and repeatedly with the divine thoughts about Christ recorded in Scripture, these good things get rooted in us and begin to produce fruit. Meditation and study of the New Testament lead to faith in Christ which leads to receiving from Christ those things that the believer needs.

Keep Your Eyes Fixed on Jesus

The results of a practiced focus on Christ might be described as "Christ-centered-ness." Christ becomes the foundation of all things in our life. He becomes our stability, our peace, our measuring rod of what is true and false, and many other things. Our inner nature, the image of Christ in us, is strengthened, and the nature of Christ is seen in us without any effort to produce it. Our mind has been renewed and has become "the mind of Christ" and we think about things much more in the way that Christ would think about them. We are able to capture and reject thoughts, attitudes, ideas, doctrines and teachings that are contrary to what Christ taught and demonstrated. We rely on, without needing measured thought, intuitively, the work of the Spirit of Christ in us.

When a believer who is practiced at keeping a good focus is challenged by bad news, he or she may be momentarily alarmed but proper focus will enable them to consider this bad news through the knowledge of Christ. As a result, their inner condition will remain full of life and peace. If they do not remain full of life and peace, it can be reacquired. They need to strengthen their focus on Christ and His answers to them to change this. Meditation on Him in the New Testament will accomplish this.

Beyond just producing life and peace within, a proper focus allows believers to live the life of the Spirit rather than the life of the flesh. The terms "spirit" and "flesh" are placed opposite each other many times in the New Testament. They are often used to compare the two ways that a believer can live. They can live by the spirit or they can live by the flesh. Paul warns Christians about this by writing:

Keep Your Eyes Fixed on Jesus

But I say, walk by the Spirit, and you will not carry out the desire of the flesh. For the flesh sets its desire against the Spirit, and the Spirit against the flesh; for these are in opposition to one another, so that you may not do the things that you please. (Galatians 5:16 -17)

The term "flesh" is translated from the Greek word "sarx" and it appears 126 times in the New Testament. It should not be confused with the Greek word translated "body". That word is "soma." The Greek word "sarx" represents that fallen part of human beings that exists before and after they receive the new nature. That new nature is often referred to as "spirit" in the New Testament. This is not to be confused with the Holy Spirit. Human beings are essentially a spirit with a soul and a body. When we are born spiritually, our spirit is brought back to life through the indwelling presence of the Holy Spirit. The "sarx" does not disappear when we become Christians. When we abide in Christ, it is crucified with Christ and has no effect on us. When we live apart from Christ, it has a profound effect on us. Theological denial that the "sarx" still exists does not change the fact that those same people will still experience the "flesh" if their focus is wrong.

The capacity of a Christian to "walk by the Spirit" or by "the desire of the flesh" is apparent. You simply cannot do both at the same time. Walking "by the Spirit" is not automatic. It is a matter of focus and sometimes requires a strong decision to deny the desire of the flesh. If our focus is fleshly, earthly, we will carry out the desire of the flesh. If it is spiritual, our new nature in Christ will be activated and we will walk by the power of the Holy Spirit refreshing and invigorating our spirits.

Keep Your Eyes Fixed on Jesus

Paul warns that no Christian "may do the things that they please." In another place, he reminds that living according to the flesh will produce death but living according to the Spirit will mean putting to death the sinful deeds of the body. This will produce life in a believer.

...if you are living according to the flesh, you must die; but if by the Spirit you are putting to death the deeds of the body, you will live. (Romans 8:13)

The New Testament draws a strong distinction between living in the flesh and living in the Spirit repeatedly for believers. It warns us that if we walk in the flesh, we will reap very bad results. Obviously, the sin nature, the flesh, "sarx", can still be a serious problem to believers or Paul would not warn believers about it. Paul writes in another place:

For the one who sows to his own flesh shall from the flesh reap corruption, but the one who sows to the Spirit shall from the Spirit reap eternal life. Galatians 6:8

Paul offers a serious warning and a wonderful promise in the same verse. Sowing the flesh will cause us to reap corruption. The Greek word translated as "corruption" here is "phthora". It is often translated as "destruction." On the other hand, Paul tells us that sowing "to the Spirit" will cause us to reap "eternal life". It is noteworthy that Paul does not assume that "eternal life" is an automatic result of being a Christian. He warns of the possibility of another result. So learning how to keep our eyes fixed on Jesus and walking by the Spirit are not only profitable but will ensure that we experience everything that God has for us. Thankfully, it will also ensure that we do not

Keep Your Eyes Fixed on Jesus

experience the things that Christ and His apostles warn about. Keep your eyes fixed on Jesus!

Inexpensive Materials for Meditation on Christ. Because Christians are often relatively inexperienced in keeping a focus on Christ, and often do not know specifically what to focus upon, the author has created some resources that are specifically created for this purpose available on www.allnationsmin.org.

Healing Meditation Cards. These playing cards have 104 Christ Centered verses, meditations and confessions concerning healing. They are designed to move Christians from intellectual acceptance that God heals to simple and personal faith in Christ as their Healer.

Identity in Christ Meditation Cards. These playing cards have 104 Christ centered verses, meditations and confessions concerning our identity in Christ. They are designed to help Christians develop a strong self image based on who they are in Christ.

Spiritual Focus Meditation Cards. These playing cards have 104 Christ centered verses meditation and confessions. They create a strong focus on Christ that will enable believers to live in the new nature empowered by the Holy Spirit.

A Christ centered meditation card game called "Grace and Glory" is available as a free download on **www.allnationsmin.org**.

Printed in Great Britain
by Amazon